DAREDEVIL SPORTS

PARKOUR

By Demi Jackson

Please visit our website, www.garethstevens.com. For a free color catalog of all our high-quality books, call toll free 1-800-542-2595 or fax 1-877-542-2596.

Cataloging-in-Publication Data

Jackson, Demi.
Parkour / by Demi Jackson.
p. cm. — (Daredevil sports)
Includes index.
ISBN 978-1-4824-2993-0 (pbk.)
ISBN 978-1-4824-2996-1 (6 pack)
ISBN 978-1-4824-2994-7 (library binding)
1. Extreme sports — Juvenile literature. 2. Parkour — Juvenile literature. I. Jackson, Demi. II. Title.
GV749.7 J34 2016
796.04'6—d23

First Edition

Published in 2016 by
Gareth Stevens Publishing
111 East 14th Street, Suite 349
New York, NY 10003

Designer: Samantha DeMartin
Editor: Kristen Rajczak

Photo credits: Cover, p. 1© iStockphoto.com/Thomas_EyeDesign; pp. 5, 7 Lars Baron/ Bongarts/Getty Images; p. 9 Sean Gallup/Getty Images Sport/Getty Images; p. 11 David S. Holloway/Getty Images News/Getty Images; p. 13 Dan Kitwood/Getty Images News/Getty Images; p. 15 Mark Ralston/AFP/Getty Images; p. 17 Paul Gilham/Getty Images Sport/Getty Images; p. 19 Quinn Rooney/Getty Images Sport/ Getty Images; pp. 21, 27 PYMCA/Universal Images Group/Getty Images; p. 23 Mahmud Turkia/AFP/Getty Images; p. 25 Cameron Spencer/Getty Images Sport/ Getty Images; p. 29 Thomas_EyeDesign/E+/Getty Images.

Printed in the United States of America

CPSIA compliance information: Batch # CS15GS: For further information contact Gareth Stevens, New York, New York at 1-800-542-2595.

CONTENTS

OVER, UNDER, AND THROUGH

When most runners see a low wall or other **obstacle** in their way, they simply go around it. But some run up the wall and jump over without stopping at all! This thrilling way of moving is called parkour (pahr-KOOR).

RISK FACTOR

A man who practices parkour is called a *traceur* (truh-SUHR). A woman who practices parkour is called a *traceuse* (truh-SUHS).

Parkour doesn't have a set of rules. One *traceur* might describe it differently than another. But generally, parkour is a way of moving from one point to another in the most **efficient** way possible. That includes going over and through obstacles!

A NEW SPORT

David Belle, a French actor and stuntman, invented parkour during the 1980s and 1990s. His father had been an **acrobat** and a fireman, and he **inspired** Belle's movement style. Parkour became known when people began to see videos made by Belle and his friends.

RISK FACTOR

Parkour was also inspired by a style of military training used in France called *parcours di combattant*.

Parkour didn't catch on in the United States until around 2000. Belle and his *traceurs* were more interested in getting better at parkour than spreading the word. Even today, parkour is much more popular in Europe than in the United States.

RISK FACTOR

Mark Toorock, founder of the American Parkour website, was one of the first to bring parkour to daredevils in the United States.

FREERUNNING

Sometimes parkour is called freerunning. *Traceur* Sebastien Foucan first created the word to describe parkour to people who speak English. Freerunners also run, jump, and climb through their neighborhoods. But over time, freerunning has become separate from parkour.

RISK FACTOR

Foucan was the freerunner featured in the beginning of the James Bond movie *Casino Royale*!

Freerunning and parkour have a key difference. Freerunning more often includes flips and other **gymnastics** moves than parkour. Freerunners value creativity above all, while Belle has said that parkour should have a use other than "doing things to look good."

RISK FACTOR

Daredevil athletes often try parkour because it's not just hard on the body, it's **mentally difficult, too.**

15

CAN YOU DO IT?

In the past, most people learned how to do parkour by watching videos on the Internet. Today, you can find classes teaching parkour to all ages! Kids as young as 3 can go to gyms set up specifically for doing parkour.

RISK FACTOR

The World Freerunning & Parkour Federation is one group that's working to bring parkour and freerunning to more people around the world.

If you sign up for a parkour class, you won't be running up walls the first day! A lot of classes teach the ideas behind parkour first. They try to inspire new *traceurs* to see the whole world as a playground to move through.

RISK FACTOR

The only gear you need for parkour is a pair of sneakers with good grip on the bottom—though kneepads are a good idea for beginners!

START SMALL

You can learn jumps and other common parkour moves in a parkour class. However, it's important for beginner *traceurs* to start small. For example, you'll try to jump off a curb before a wall of any kind!

RISK FACTOR

You can wear what you want when doing parkour! Loose-fitting clothing is often recommended.

The best *traceurs* need to be very fit to complete their movements well. They need full-body strength as well as flexibility, or the ability to bend well. Many *traceurs* have a background in martial arts or gymnastics.

RISK FACTOR

Parkour takes a lot of practice. Don't try the moves you
see in online videos without training well first.

TRUE DAREDEVIL

As the inventor of parkour, David Belle is known for his incredible parkour moves. He has videos of himself jumping over cars, landing on thin railings when leaping over stairs, and more. Belle even jumps between buildings many stories tall!

RISK FACTOR

Big moves can lead to big injuries such as
broken bones and bad bruises.

PARKOUR PARKS

You can try to do parkour anywhere! Some cities are building special parks especially for the daredevils who want to practice it. The largest outdoor parkour park in the world is in London, England. Copenhagen, Denmark, has at least five parks created for public parkour practice!

RISK FACTOR

Some parks in the United States have signs stating "No Parkour." That may change as more people start to practice the sport!

NEW LIMITS

The most important part of parkour is testing your limits! How fast can you move across your backyard without touching the grass? Trying parkour may help you find new strength and creativity you didn't know you had!

RISK FACTOR

Parkour is a fairly new sport in the United States, but it's definitely catching on!

PARKOUR SAFETY TIPS

- Master basic moves before trying anything harder.

- Try new moves on the ground or low walls first.

- Learn how to land safely. A good landing is a quiet one.

- Wear shoes that fit well and have bottoms with a good grip.

- Stay fit in other ways.

- Be mindful of where you practice. Watch for cars and other people.

FOR MORE INFORMATION

BOOKS

Mason, Paul, and Sarah Eason. *Free Running*. Minneapolis, MN: Lerner Publications, 2012.

Pipe, Jim. *Extreme Sports*. Mankato, MN: Smart Apple Media, 2012.

WEBSITES

Parkour for Beginners: 5 Moves You Can Master Quickly
news.discovery.com/adventure/extreme-sports/parkour-for-beginners-5-moves-you-can-master-quickly.htm
Ready to do tricks? This article helps you take the next steps in parkour.

What Is Parkour and Why Should Kids Do It?
kidsoutandabout.com/content/what-parkour-and-why-should-kids-do-it
Learn more about parkour and watch a video of young people explaining it.

GLOSSARY

acrobat: someone who performs gymnastics

efficient: having to do with the most effective or purposeful way of doing something

gymnastics: a sport that includes rolls, flips, and other moves often performed on rings or bars

inspire: to cause someone to want to do something

mentally: having to do with the mind

obstacle: something that blocks a path

INDEX